I WANT TO KNOW

Are Mermaids Real?

Portia Summers and
Dana Meachen Rau

Enslow Publishing
101 W. 23rd Street
Suite 240
New York, NY 10011
USA

enslow.com

Published in 2017 by Enslow Publishing, LLC
101 W. 23rd St., Suite 240, New York, NY 10011

Library of Congress Cataloging-in-Publication Data

Names: Summers, Portia, author.
Title: Are mermaids real? / Portia Summers and Dana Meachen Rau.
Description: New York : Enslow Publishing, 2016. | Series: I want to know | Includes bibliographical references and index.
Identifiers: LCCN 2016024751| ISBN 9780766082427 (library bound) | ISBN 9780766082403 (pbk.) | ISBN 9780766082410 (6-pack)
Subjects: LCSH: Mermaids—Juvenile literature.
Classification: LCC GR910 .S86 2016 | DDC 398.21—dc23
LC record available at https://lccn.loc.gov/2016024751

Printed in China

To Our Readers: We have done our best to make sure all websites in this book were active and appropriate when we went to press. However, the author and the publisher have no control over and assume no liability for the material available on those websites or on any websites they may link to. Any comments or suggestions can be sent by email to customerservice@ enslow.com.

Photo Credits: Cover, p. 3 © iStockphoto.com/CoreyFord; p. 4 zhudifeng/iStock/Thinkstock; p. 5 Leemage/Universal Images Group/Getty Images; p. 6 SeM/Universal Images Group/Bridgeman Images; p. 7 David Fleetham/Taxi/Getty Images; p. 9 © Fine Art Images/SuperStock; p. 10 superjoseph/iStock/Thinkstock; p. 11 Everett-Art/Shutterstock.com; p. 13 Peter O'Toole/Shutterstock.com; p. 14 Toby Adams/Design Pics/Axiom Photographic Agency/Getty Images; p. 15 Everett Historical/Shutterstock.com; p. 16 tobaisfrei/iStock/Thinkstock;p. 17 Andria Patino/Corbis Documentary/Getty Images; p. 19 Coqrouge/Shutterstock.com; p. 20 Vinicius Tupinamba/Shutterstock.com; p. 21 Vilainecrevette/Shutterstock.com; p. 22 J Need/Shutterstock.com; p. 23 Raymond Gehman/Corbis Documentary/Getty Images; p. 24 Kathryn Scott Osler/The Denver Post/Getty Images; p. 25 Alex Pix/Shutterstock.com; p. 28 Alan Poulson/Shutterstock.com.

Contents

Chapter 1

· · · · · · · · · ·

Seeing the Seas

For hundreds of years, sailors and explorers watched the ocean from the decks of their ships. Sometimes, creatures from below the water came to the surface. Lively dolphins jumped alongside the ship. Huge whales came up from the depths to breathe. Many worried about sea monsters. Sailors watched the water around their ships for these monsters.

Imagine That!

Cartographers, or mapmakers, drew dragons, mermaids, and sea monsters in the oceans on their maps.

People from the Sea

Some of these sailors claimed to see people in the water. But these people weren't other sailors who had jumped overboard. They wrote stories about these surprising creatures that had upper bodies like humans. But instead of legs, these creatures had long, scaly fish tails. They called these creatures mermaids and mermen.

Ancient Mermaids

The first ever (1000 BCE) story of a mermaid is the Syrian story of Atargatis, who wanted to become a fish after her lover had died. But the gods refused to turn her into a fish because she was so beautiful. So they turned only her bottom half.

But even older than that are stories of mermen. The first merman was the Babylonian god Oannes (ca. 8000 BCE). According to myth, Oannes had the head of a man and the body of a fish and would come to the seashore to teach mankind about writing, arts and sciences.

Stories of mermaids and mermen have been told since people started sailing the seas. Tales came from northern countries near cold water, such as Iceland and Denmark. Stories also came from warm southern islands, such as Polynesia and the Caribbean. The further explorers travelled, the more they shared the stories of their adventures and the things they had seen. Mermaid stories from different countries mixed together.

Many sailors exchanged stories about beautiful women with fish tails who lived in the watery depths of the ocean.

Chapter 2

. . . .

Oceans of Stories

Many mermaid tales told of magnificent underwater kingdoms where the beautiful creatures lived. The mermaids would swim to the surface and lay out on rocks. Often they were described combing their long hair, admiring their reflections, and wearing pearls from the sea. Some were described as beautiful with pale skin. Others were said to have green or blue skin and hair.

Mermaid Magic

In many stories, mermaids had special powers. Some could grant wishes. Some could tell the future. Others could **hypnotize** sailors into following them below the waves. Many mermaids were dangerous, **luring**

Mermaids were said to sit on rocks and comb their hair or lure sailors from their ships with songs.

unsuspecting sailors to their deaths. The ancient Greeks told stories of **sirens**. Sirens are similar to mermaids, except that it is their beautiful singing voices that bewitch sailors. These stories stated that the sirens' song could cause an entire fleet of ships to wreck against the rocks.

Many shipwrecks were blamed on mermaids and sirens.

Imagine That!

Mermaids are not the only women of the sea. The Greek goddess Aphrodite [Afro-di-tee] emerged from the sea in a clam shell. The Assyrian goddess Asatarte [Ah-sat-art-ay] and the African goddess Mamiwata also emerged from the sea. All three were goddesses of love, beauty, and destruction.

Mermaids Around the World

Mermaid stories came from all over the world. Ancient Greeks told many stories about gods. Triton, a god of the sea, was a merman. He carried a horn made of a **conch** shell. When he blew it, he could make storms on the ocean, which were dangerous for sailors.

The Irish and Scots told tales of mermaids called merrows who wore magical caps that let them swim deep to a dry kingdom hidden under the sea. Merrows often fell in love with fishermen. If their red caps were stolen, they couldn't return to the sea.

Explorers brought their stories of mermaids to the New World. Christopher Columbus claimed to have seen many on his crossing of the Atlantic. John Smith also claimed to have seen one on his **voyage**. The mermaid goddess of the Caribbean and Latin America is Lasirèn [La-sir-EN]. Like other mermaids, she sits on rocks combing her hair and admiring her reflection.

In Haiti, she is an important part of **Voodoo** tradition. Followers pray to her for good luck with work, health, money, and love.

Imagine That!

Perhaps the most famous story of mermaids is Danish writer Hans Christian Andersen's *The Little Mermaid* (later adapted into a film by Disney). The story tells of a mermaid who falls in love with a human prince and gives up her voice in order to be with him. The story is so well known that there is even a statue of the little mermaid in the harbor in Copenhagen, Denmark.

Sedna, also known as Arnakuagsak (ar-NAK-oog-SAK), was an important goddess in Inuit mythology, making sure that the fishermen caught enough fish to feed their people.

The Inuit people of Canada and Greenland tell a story of Sedna, who was a young woman tossed overboard by her father. She survived to create the whales, seals, and walruses that the Inuit relied on to survive.

Chapter 3

Serious Sightings

Christopher Columbus claimed to have seen mermaids in the Caribbean in 1493. He described them as ugly. Henry Hudson, another famous explorer, claimed to see a mermaid in the icy northern waters off Russia in 1608, too. This mermaid was described as having long black hair and white skin.

Mermaids or Marine Mammals?

Some people think the mermaids Columbus and other sailors saw may have been **manatees** or **dugongs**. Dugongs live in the Indian and South Pacific oceans. Manatees live in the southern Atlantic. Both of these mammals live in warm shallow water and eat sea grass. They must come to the surface of the water to breathe. They have long, fat, gray bodies, and they use short

Manatees are thought to have been mistaken for mermaids by sailors who were unfamiliar with the marine life in warm climates.

Mermaids, Mermaids, Everywhere!

Mermaids are still an important part of our **culture**. They have been used in advertisements and as **mascots**. They are depicted in sculptures and art in sea-side towns across the world. They have been in films, television shows, and books. The mermaid is even a part of the city of Warsaw, Poland's coat of arms.

Every year at Coney Island in New York City, there is a mermaid parade. People dress up like mermaids and other fantastical creatures to celebrate the beginning of summer.

flippers and flat tails to swim. Henry Hudson could not have seen a manatee or dugong. He was exploring cold, icy waters where these mammals can't live. So what did he and his men see? Maybe they saw seals or walruses. But these sailors knew ocean creatures well from all of their travels, and would have recognized a seal or a walrus.

A Sailor's Sights

How could they mistake a common seal or walrus for a mermaid? Remember, a sailor from long ago would have had to work very hard day and night. They wouldn't see their families or homes for months (or sometimes years) at a time. Some ships weren't stocked with enough food and water to feed their crews. Dim light before electricity would have made it hard to see. A long figure with a tail ducking beneath the surface of the water could easily be mistaken for a mermaid.

Having the figure of a mermaid on a ship's front was meant to protect its crew from the dangers of the sea.

Imagine That!

Legend states that the gem aquamarine is made when a mermaid cries.

It wasn't hard for explorers to believe mermaids could be real. They were seeing new sights all the time. Maybe they really saw manatees, dugongs, seals, or walruses. Maybe they just liked to tell good stories, like fishermen still do today.

Chapter 4
. . . .

In Search of Mermaids

Today, most people accept that mermaids are merely the subject of sailor's imaginations. Oceans cover about three quarters of the Earth. **Oceanographers** and **marine biologists** have not fully explored all of them yet. The more they explore, the more they discover. But so far, they haven't found any mermaids.

Imagine That!

A mermaid's purse is really a skate's **egg case**. A skate is a type of fish.

Many "mermaids" perform at water and theme parks around the world, like this one at Weeki Wachee Springs in Florida.

Modern Mermaids

Many people, however, still believe, or at very least, are fans of mermaids. There are many artists who dress themselves as mermaids (including tails!) and perform shows in the water.

There are even special schools where these artists will teach you how to swim, jump, and dance in the water like a mermaid!

Fiji Mermaid

In 1842, famed circus creator P.T. Barnum began displaying the body of a mermaid in his museum. The small, **mummified** creature was an extremely popular exhibit. But it turned out to be a fake. Instead of a beautiful woman with the tail of a fish, the Fiji Mermaid was the head and body of a monkey connected to the body of a fish.

Just because scientists haven't found proof of mermaids doesn't mean they don't exist, or that they never did. Mermaids have become legends in cultures across the world. There are paintings of them in caves from 30,000 years ago and even images of them in old Bibles. Maybe mermaids existed at one time. Or maybe, they're simply living quietly in an uncharted corner of the ocean.

Words to Know

adapt To adjust something to make it suitable for film or stage.

cartographer A person who creates maps.

conch [KONK] A sea animal with a spiral-shaped shell.

culture The arts, attitudes, beliefs, traditions, and other achievements of humans.

dugong A mammal with a fat body, short flippers, and a flat dolphin-like tail that lives in the Indian and South Pacific oceans.

egg case A pouch or sac that holds an animal's eggs.

hypnotize To capture another person's whole attention.

lure To attract something closer.

manatee A mammal with a fat body, short flippers, and a flat paddle-shaped tail that lives in the southern Atlantic Ocean.

marine biologist A scientist who studies life in the ocean.

mascot A person or thing that is supposed to bring good luck to a group or team.

mummified Preserved.

oceanographer A scientist who studies the physical features of the ocean.

siren A creature with a beautiful voice that lures sailors onto the rocks.

Voodoo A religion practiced in the Caribbean and southern United States which combines Christian and traditional African beliefs.

voyage A very long journey by boat

Further Reading

Books

Berk, Ari. *The Secret History of Mermaids.* Somerville, MA: Candlewick Press, 2009.

DK Publishing. *Children's Book of Mythical Beasts and Magical Monsters.* New York, NY: Penguin Random House, 2011.

Rizzo, Johanna. *Oceans: Dolphins, Sharks, Penguins, and More!* Washington, D.C.: National Geographic Kids. 2010.

Scamander, Newt. *Fantastic Beasts and Where to Find Them (Harry Potter).* New York, NY: Arthur A. Levine Books, 2015.

Websites

American Museum of Natural History

www.amnh.org/exhibitions/mythic-creatures/water-creatures-of-the-deep/becoming-mermaids/

Learn more about mermaid mythology from around the world.

Discovery Kids

discoverykids.com/videos/how-to-swim-with-manatees/

Learn how to swim like a manatee!

Smithsonian National Museum of Natural History

ocean.si.edu/ocean-news/mermaids-manatees-myth-and-reality

Read more about mermaids and manatees.

Index

About the Authors

Portia Summers is an adventurer who loves stories. She has traveled the world in search of the truth behind legends. She has searched for gargoyles in Italy, elves in Ireland, and mermaids in Israel. She has written many books on many different subjects, and hopes she can continue to do so for a long time. She lives in New York City, where she is sure that gremlins help keep her computer up-to-date.

Dana Meachen Rau is the author of more than 250 books for children. She has written about many nonfiction topics from her home office. Mrs. Rau has never seen a mermaid, but she did see a humpback whale breach the surface of the water off Cape Cod.

DATE DUE

			PRINTED IN U.S.A.